WORTHY IN JESUS

UNOFFICIAL STUDY & DISCUSSION GUIDE
FOR *THE GIFTS OF IMPERFECTION*

by LEAH PRITCHARD

Gideon House Books
www.gideonhousebooks.com

Scripture references marked (NASB) are taken from the *New American Standard Bible*, © 1960, 1963, 1968, 1971, 1972, 1973, 1975, 1977 by The Lockman Foundation. Used by permission.

Scripture quotations marked (NIV) are taken from the Holy Bible, *New International Version*®. NIV®. Copyright© 1973, 1978, 1984 by International Bible Society. Used by permission of Zondervan. All rights reserved.

Scripture taken from the *New King James Version*. Copyright © 1982 by Thomas Nelson, Inc. Used by permission. All rights reserved.

ISBN: 978-1-943133-23-9

Gideon House Books
http://www.gideonhousebooks.com

To Nancy,
my counselor and mentor,
whom God has used quietly and mightily to renew my mind
and plant many of the truths found in this study guide deep inside my heart.

Contents

Introduction

I stumbled upon Brené Brown's *The Gifts of Imperfection* by "chance" one day in the middle of a particularly chaotic period in my life. My husband was wrapping up his 4-year seminary degree which had taken us 6 years to complete. We were still getting used to life as a family of 4 with the arrival of our second child. At the same time we were preparing to move ourselves, our newborn daughter, our 3-year-old son and our business overseas.

Our little family was living in a temporary, roach-infested apartment above raucous downstairs neighbors and I found myself struggling with postpartum depression. It had snuck up on me and knocked me off balance at the most inconvenient time imaginable. There was so much to be done!

Life was crazy and there were some days we weren't sure if we were going to survive the next day, never mind a move across the ocean.

God had my attention. I had been so certain this move was His plan for our family, but now my mind was clouded with doubts. If He wanted us to make this big move, He was going to have to be the One to pull it off.

He *did* want us to make the move, and He wanted us to do it His way.

First He wanted to teach me the importance of rest, something essential if I was going to survive life in a new culture. Physical, emotional and spiritual rest. He wanted to teach me how to take good care of myself. I had always worked hard to love others, but now I was struck with how little I understood how to love myself. I also needed to learn how to walk slowly, one day at a time, so I could experience and access the strength He had waiting for me in each moment, so I could see His glorious power at work in me.

As I found myself weak and struggling with the postpartum depression, unable to do everything I wanted to do and suddenly unsure about my future, many of the fears and insecurities I had struggled with my entire life came to a head and taunted me.

When it felt like an uphill battle for me to get the dishwasher unloaded, forget about anything else, I was scared. Who was I when I couldn't accomplish anything? I was a hard worker, a doer, an accomplisher.

God showed me that all my life I had been finding my worth and identity in what I could do and what I could accomplish; and in my ability to "keep myself pulled together." That was not the identity He wanted for me.

He began to whisper His most sacred secrets to my soul.

He showed me my worth isn't dependent on what I do or what I accomplish for myself, for the world or for Him. He rocked me in His arms and told me I was just as worthy in His sight when I was curled up helplessly in my bed while my mother-in-law watched my kids as when I was powerfully leading a Bible study or sharing my faith with friends. My worth is based in Him alone and in what He has done for me; not in anything I do.

I am *worthy in Jesus.*

One afternoon during this time I reached my daily limit for sorting toys and packing boxes so I sank down into the couch and popped open my laptop to take a little break. Somehow I found myself perusing down a reading list posted by an online book club. The title of *The Gifts of Imperfection* immediately caught my eye. I threw it in my Amazon shopping cart and started reading it that same afternoon.

I had no idea what a jewel of a book I had found or how God would use this secular book to reinforce in my heart all He had been teaching me that spring.

Brown's book is the kind of book meant to be read slowly, carefully and thoughtfully; but the first time through I just devoured it. I kept reading and reading. I let all her wise, thoughtful insights and the personal stories from her life splash me full in the face. It was absolutely brilliant.

When I finished, I sat down and typed the following note to my three closest friends:

March 21, 2014

Bethany, Katy & Laurie,

Okay so what is going on with me is that God is continuing to CLEAN HOUSE in my heart before we leave for Asia. It has just continued to be wild. I can't even express it all. I am being transformed into a new person. He keeps freeing me from things I didn't even know I needed to be freed from. It is very painful but it is breathtaking when I sit and think about all God has done in the past 3 months. The Enemy keeps flinging reasons at us why we are not qualified for the work He has called us to do. He keeps flinging lies, fear, temptation. God keeps taking those one at a time and extinguishing them and showing us we are nothing without Him and everything with Him.

I just read a book called The Gifts of Imperfection *and have never highlighted so many quotes in a book before in my life. It basically talks about lots of things I've been learning the past several years but for me brought it all to a deeper layer. It is inspiring to read and PAINFUL to put into practice. All about being vulnerable and real and authentic and dealing with the shame and fear that tries to keep us from those good things. Whew. I never realized before that I have "shame attacks" but now I do. Most of the time they come from fear of being rejected if I am vulnerable and show people the real me. After I share something personal I sometimes have a shame attack because I am so afraid of what people will think.*

Anyway, this book has really sparked a ton of thought, discussion and openness in our house so I wanted to share it with you. Someone please read it and join me in this painful liberation.

I love you all,
me

A year after writing this letter we had made it to Asia and I found myself delving into Brown's book once again; this time more slowly. I led a discussion group on the book for some expat friends and our study spanned across several months.

Multiple times in *The Gifts of Imperfection* Brown talks about faith and spirituality. Her book is a beautifully written, well-researched, invaluable resource; but it is not a Christian book and it is not linked to the Bible in any way. Both times I read the book I found myself continuously pausing to consider how my Christian faith and biblical beliefs aligned with what the author was sharing.

Our discussion group in Asia was comprised of all Christians and we were interested in exploring together the connections between Brown's work and what God was speaking to our hearts through His Word. Drawing comparisons between the truths Brown discovered through her research and the Truth found in the infallible Word of God brought the fruits of Brown's research and writing to an even deeper level in our hearts.

When a concept finds its anchor in God's Word it takes on a whole new life.

"For the word of God is living and powerful, and sharper than any two-edged sword, piercing even to the division of soul and spirit, and of joints and marrow, and is a discerner of the thoughts and intents of the heart." Hebrews 4:12

This study guide you hold in your hands is designed to do two things.

First, it provides thought-provoking questions that will guide you through a thorough self-reflection and fascinating group discussion of Brené Brown's wonderful best-selling book The Gifts of Imperfection.

Second, Worthy in Jesus will take you a step further as we explore together what the Bible has to say about the different concepts and ideas presented in Brown's book.

Worthy in Jesus is not a stand-alone study; it is designed specifically to go along with Brown's book The Gifts of Imperfection. Any time I reference "the author" or page numbers I am referencing Brené Brown and page numbers which align with both print and Kindle versions of *The Gifts of Imperfection*. Each chapter in this study guide corresponds with a chapter in *The Gifts of Imperfection*.

I wish to thank Brené Brown from the bottom of my heart for her groundbreaking and tenacious research, for her stunning book and for her courageous vulnerability in sharing herself with all of us through its pages. God has absolutely used her book to challenge my thinking and change my life. I am grateful.

My prayer for each of you, as you make your way through this study guide, is that God will do something brand new in your heart. May you come away with newfound freedom, fresh joy and a beautiful lightness in your heart.

May we all learn together just how *Worthy* we are *in Jesus*.

Suggested Guidelines For Group Discussion

As you go through this study as part of a discussion group you will have opportunity for self-reflection and for sharing the fruits of your reflection with your peers.

In order to create and maintain a positive experience and safe environment for everyone in your group I recommend implementing the following guidelines during your discussion times:

1. Everyone is always encouraged to share, but no one is ever forced to share. It is always okay to say "I'll pass on this one."

2. Affirm each other when you share with a simple "Thank you, [name]." or "Thank you for sharing that."

3. Avoid interrupting one another or arguing with someone else's experience.

4. Avoid trying to "fix" one another.

5. Remember that each person's story is his or her own to share. Unless express permission is granted (or someone is in danger, of course) what is shared in the group stays in the group.

6. Enjoy your journey together!

"Courage, Compassion & Connection: The Gifts of Imperfection"

Questions for Reflection & Discussion

Recognizing Shame (pp. 7-9)

1. According to the author, what does shame feel like physically?

2. How do the following verses depict the physical aspect of the feeling of shame?

Ezra 9:6

Psalm 69:7

Jeremiah 6:15

Daniel 9:8

3. Look ahead briefly to pages 40-41 in The Gifts of Imperfection. What is the difference between guilt and shame?

Shame. It's a basic human emotion, and one we all experience. Some of us feel it more often and more acutely than others due to false messages we believe, but shame touches each and every one of us.

When God created us it was never His intention for us to experience the pain of shame.

In Genesis 2:25-3:10 we find the birth story of shame.

2:25 And they were both naked, the man and his wife, and were not ashamed.

3:1 Now the serpent was more cunning than any beast of the field which the Lord God had made. And he said to the woman, "Has God indeed said, 'You shall not eat of every tree of the garden'?" **2** And the woman said to the serpent, "We may eat the fruit of the trees of the garden; **3** but of the fruit of the tree which is in the midst of the garden, God has said, 'You shall not eat it, nor shall you touch it, lest you die.'" **4** Then the serpent said to the woman, "You will not surely die. **5** For God knows that in the day you eat of it your eyes will be opened, and you will be like God, knowing good and evil." **6** So when the woman saw that the tree was good for food, that it was pleasant to the eyes, and a tree desirable to make one wise, she took of its fruit and ate. She also gave to her husband with her, and he ate. **7** Then the eyes of both of them were opened, and they knew that they were naked; and they sewed fig leaves together and made themselves coverings.

8 And they heard the sound of the Lord God walking in the garden in the cool of the day, and Adam and his wife hid themselves from the presence of the Lord God among the trees of the garden. **9** Then the Lord God called to Adam and said to him, "Where are you?" **10** So he said, "I heard Your voice in the garden, and I was afraid because I was naked; and I hid myself."

In the very beginning, there was no shame. Genesis 2:25 says, "And they were both naked, the man and his wife, and *were. not. ashamed.*"

They had no reason to be ashamed because after God created the first man and the first woman He said they were good. (See Genesis 1:31.) *Good.* They lacked nothing. They were complete and fully accepted by God and by one another. They were *enough*. And they knew it. They believed it. They believed what God said about them was true.

They believed it until, that is, a slick snake slithered over and suggested otherwise. In 3:5 the serpent raises a new idea they had never considered before. He whispers in their ears for the very first time, *you are not enough.*

There's more you could be. More you should be! If you eat this fruit, then you will finally actually be enough. Then you will see all things and you will be like God.

Tragically, the woman believed the serpent's lie. She listened to his seductive little voice. She believed she was not enough—that she could be more!—and reached for the fruit. She bit it, she shared it with her man; and everything changed.

Bitter, ugly sin barged into the world and darkness enveloped their very souls.

So did shame.

Did you catch it? In verse 2:25 we read they were naked and unashamed. But take a look at 3:8. Their blissful unashamedness has vanished. Instead what we see is a pressing, painful awareness that there is something very, very wrong with them. They feel shame, and immediately they dive for the bushes to hide.

Ironically enough what the serpent had originally whispered as a lie, "You are not enough! You could be more!" had now come true. Now they *really were* not enough. Because of their sin, they had fallen from "enoughness." They no longer measured up to God's perfect standard of goodness.

4. Shame whispers accusingly in our ears, "You're not good enough." "There's something wrong with you." "Who do you think you are?" Read Romans 3:23. According to God's Word, what is wrong with every single one of us before we meet Jesus? How are we "not enough" before we accept His gift of forgiveness and salvation?

For many years in my mind I automatically connected shame with acts of sin. And it's true: When we sin and our sin is uncovered or seen by others we will almost definitely experience the feeling of shame. However, it's important to understand that because of the way sin and shame have infiltrated our fallen world, shameful feelings are not always linked to specific acts of sin.

Some of us feel shame when we make simple human mistakes or appear incompetent in front of people. We feel it when something we attempt doesn't turn out as well as we hoped, or when someone catches us "with our hair down" in an unguarded moment.

When we feel shame in these situations it is because somewhere deep inside we believe the lies that we are supposed to be perfect all the time, do everything well all the time, and "have it together" all the time; and there is "something wrong with us" when we aren't able to pull all that off and act like the imperfect human beings that we are.

We also feel shame when we open our true selves up to others and share what is personal and meaningful to us; maybe something we created, an opinion or idea, or even a Facebook post. We especially feel it when people don't respond as we hoped. We automatically and usually unconsciously assume then that we, and whatever we shared, "isn't good enough." And so the shame sneaks up.

Electric scooters are the preferred mode of transportation in the city where I live in Asia. It's not uncommon to see an entire family: mom, dad, grandma, and a kid or two, plus a live chicken about to become dinner, all balanced on a small two-wheeled scooter weaving in and out of cement trucks, buses, taxis and more scooters.

When we first moved here, the prospect of driving a scooter made my palms sweat. I couldn't picture balancing myself—let alone myself, my 3-year-old son, 9-month-old daughter and a few bags of groceries—on one of those vehicles.

But then I spotted it at a scooter shop: a *three-wheeled* scooter! Bigger and much more stable, it's the mommy minivan of electric scooters. Mine is bright red and has a pink (yes pink!) umbrella attached to keep off sun and rain. I climb onto the front seat to drive and my kids get strapped to the wide back seat, their arms and legs sprawled over grocery bags to keep the contents from spilling out into the street.

Last week I piled my kids and myself onto my wonder scooter to visit a friend who lives in an apartment complex down the road. Scooters are supposed to enter the complex through a narrow entrance gate. The gate is plenty wide for two-wheeled scooters, but my pink umbrella'd three-wheeler just barely makes it through. On this day I managed to squeeze in without scraping the sides, keenly aware of the unsmiling gate guards, puffing on their cigarettes, scrutinizing me; but when I tried to leave a few hours later I rammed one side of the gate as I passed through. *Hard.*

All the passersby heard the banging and scraping and stopped to stare. As I felt their eyes and the eyes of the gate guards on my back, I felt it rising…*shame.* My mouth went dry and my face burned.

I slowed down just long enough to look over my right shoulder and make sure I hadn't damaged the gate—I hadn't—so I floored it and kept going.

All the way home I experienced the "tunnel vision" Brown describes in her book. I kept replaying the moment and beating myself up for it. *How could I have hit the gate? I can't believe I did that. How can I ever go back to my friend's house and face those gate guards again? Oh gosh are they going to tell my friend what I did?* In my mind I could hear the gate guards in their little hut guffawing and waving their cigarettes in the air at the crazy foreign lady who doesn't know how to drive.

Somewhere along the road of life I have believed the lie that I'm supposed to be perfect all the time, and if I'm not perfect there must something wrong with me. On this day I couldn't stand the fact that I had made a mistake driving and felt shame that people had seen me do it.

Tell my husband or not tell my husband? When I got back home I was tempted to keep it to myself. Shame really does scream, "Hide me!" Unfortunately for my shame one of the back seat arms of my scooter was badly bent out of shape so I figured I may as well come clean.

Deep breath.

I told him the story.

The world didn't cave in on me and I felt better immediately. He chuckled kindly and reminded me nobody's perfect. "Don't worry about it, everybody does stuff like that sometimes."

Relieved, I went on with my day, but to this day every time I visit my friend and pass those gate guards I have to firmly remind myself that I am *worthy.*

5. Describe a time when you felt shame. What triggered the feeling? How did your body feel? What was going through your mind at the time?

Responding to Shame (pp. 9-12)

6. According to the book, what is the best thing to do when we experience the feeling of shame? (Here's a hint: It's the opposite of what Adam & Eve did when they felt shame in Genesis 3!) How easy or difficult is this for you?

7. What can we learn from the following verses about God's plan to free His children from the pain of shame?

Romans 9:33

Romans 10:11

Isaiah 61:7

Psalm 34:5

Isaiah 54:4

8. When you are sharing something personal or doing something vulnerable, what kinds of responses from friends hurt you and leave you feeling unsafe? What kinds of responses leave you feeling accepted and loved?

Living Courageously (pp. 12-15)

9. What is "ordinary courage" as the author describes it? (See pages 12, 13.)

10. Describe a time when you demonstrated "ordinary courage."

Offering Genuine Compassion (pp. 15-19)

As a recovering codependent who is prone to feeling responsible for meeting the needs of the entire universe and who believed for many years that compassion meant helping, fixing and taking care of instead of "suffering with" (see page 16), it has been a difficult lesson for me to learn that demonstrating compassion and setting boundaries are not mutually exclusive concepts.

When someone asks me to do something I don't want to do or don't have time to do, and I say *yes*, my motivation is usually not love, it's guilt; and it never bodes well. I end up angry with myself for getting into the situation and annoyed with the person who asked for my help. My heart is not full of compassion, it's full of impatience and bitterness. This is not glorifying to God.

I have from time to time been known to set forth on grand schemes to "take care of" people who are hurting. Moved by what I mistake for compassion (really it's my unrelenting drive to help, fix and rescue...to play God in someone's life) I offer to take over some task for them, or make them a meal, or give them a ride...but not just this once, oh no! I offer my ongoing assistance every week for the next six months! By week three I am inevitably weary and beginning to feel taken advantage of; I completely lose sight of the reason I initially offered to help in the first place.

We are not God, and we can't carry all the burdens of the world on our shoulders. We can't make people happy, we can't fix problems for people who are hurting. But we absolutely can suffer with them and reach out to love them from our hearts as God leads us. When we serve out of genuine desire and true love, it is a beautiful act rich with eternal value. But when our service springs from any other motivation, such as guilt or an unconscious drive to rescue and take on God's role, it is merely hay and stubble.

> "If I slip into the place that can be filled by Christ alone, making myself the first necessity to a soul instead of leading it to fasten upon Him, then I know nothing of Calvary love."—Amy Carmichael, *If*

11. How do setting boundaries* (saying no when we want or need to say no) and keeping people accountable for their actions help make us more genuinely compassionate people?

> "Before the breakdown I was sweeter—judgmental, resentful and angry on the inside—but sweeter on the outside. Today, I think I'm genuinely more compassionate, less judgmental and resentful, and way more serious about boundaries."—*The Gifts of Imperfection*, page 16

12. In what ways do you identify with this quote? How comfortable are you with setting boundaries and keeping people accountable for their actions?

Connecting Deeply (pp. 19-21)

13. What is needed for true connection to happen between people? (See page 19.)

14. How often do you ask for help? What is something you could really use some help with right now that you have been trying to do on your own?

*Recommended Reading: *Boundaries* by Dr. Henry Cloud & Dr. John Townsend

"Exploring the Power of Love, Belonging, and Being Enough"

Questions for Reflection & Discussion

Discovering Our Worthiness (pp. 23-24)

> "I realized that only *one thing* separated the men and women who felt a deep sense of love and belonging from the people who seemed to be struggling for it. That one thing is the belief in their worthiness."—*The Gifts of Imperfection*, page 23

1. What is worthiness, as described in this book?

2. What is one thing about yourself that doesn't now or hasn't in the past fit with who you think you are supposed to be or who you thought you were supposed to be?

"Worthy now. Not if. Now when. We are worthy of love and belonging now. Right this minute. As is."—*The Gifts of Imperfection*, page 24

I love this quote. It is so inspiring. So uplifting! But when I first read it I realized I needed to stop and ask a really important question: *Is it true?*

The Bible teaches that every human being has intrinsic value and worth because each of us is made in the image of God (Genesis 1:26, 27, 31). We are worthy of love because He loves us. He loves every single person in the world (John 3:16). Our worthiness doesn't come from ourselves, it comes from the One who created us and the One who loves us; the One who alone is worthy to receive blessing and honor and glory and power (Revelation 5:12, 13).

He has built it into us, this undeniable value and worth, and whether we believe in God or not I believe we can all discover and tap into a certain depth of it. However, we can only take it so far without God. Without Him we're merely grasping at air as we search for something solid in which to anchor our worthiness.

Our sin nature poses a real problem when it comes to our worthiness. We have intrinsic value and worth, and God loves us; but the truth is that because of our sin nature we're *not* worthy.

We're *not* worthy of acceptance. We're *not* worthy of belonging. And although God loves us, our sin nature blocks our access to the vast riches of His Fatherly love. We are *not* worthy of experiencing His love on a deep and personal level.

The first half of Romans 6:23 tells us, "The wages of sin is death." The eternal death this is referring to means eternal separation or *not belonging*. After Adam and Eve sinned, they were no longer worthy of God's acceptance. They didn't belong in the Garden with Him any more. In Genesis 3:23, 24 we read that God sent Adam and Eve away. He sent them away from the Garden and away from His close and loving presence. Because they had sinned, they were no longer worthy. And they knew it; they were ashamed.

Thankfully for all of us, this isn't even close to the end of the story. God had a plan from the very beginning that could restore each and every one of us to our full place of worthiness before Him. The second half of Romans 6:23 tells us this plan: "The wages of sin is death, *but the gift of God is eternal life in Jesus Christ our Lord.*"

God sent Jesus, His perfect Son, into the world to die in our place and take the punishment we deserve. When Jesus died on the cross His own Father turned His back on Him (Matthew 27:46) and Jesus experienced the separation from God that *we* deserve.

He, the only Worthy One, died for us so that we can be completely worthy—worthy of love, belonging and acceptance—to God. The Bible tells us after He died He came back to life! He rose from the dead to show His power and victory over sin and death and shame.

Jesus offers His worthiness as a gift to anyone who will believe and accept it. The gift is not based on anything we do or how good we are (see Ephesians 2:8, 9). Rather, it is based completely on the fact that Jesus Christ, the sinless Son of God, died in our place on the cross to restore us to a place of complete worthiness in the eyes of God. He offers us a place of love, belonging and acceptance in His family forever.

3. Have you ever accepted the free gift of eternal life God offers to everyone who believes in Jesus? If you never have, would you like to right now? All you need to do is talk to God and let Him know. He hears you! Say something like this:

> "God, here I am. I believe You're here with me right now. I know there is sin in my life and I understand my sinfulness makes me unworthy and unacceptable in Your sight. Please forgive me for all my sins—past, present and future. Please wash me clean and make me 100% worthy now and forever through Your Son Jesus Christ. I believe Jesus died in my place to pay the penalty for my sins. I believe He came back to life to conquer sin and shame once and for all. I want to accept Your free gift of salvation right now. Thank you, Lord!"

Welcome to the family! If you have accepted God's gift by "confessing with your mouth the Lord Jesus and believing in your heart that God has raised Him from the dead" (Romans 10:9), the Bible says you are now and forever a child of God, loved and accepted in His eyes. You are **Worthy in Jesus!**

If you have accepted this gift (just now or previously in your life) write out a prayer to God expressing your gratitude for His amazing gift:

Once we are children of God, it becomes our daily path to joy and freedom to follow Him and to increasingly claim and live out of the fact that we are indeed worthy of God's love and belonging *now*, just as we are, because of Jesus.

He has traded in our filthy garments that were stained with sin for clean robes that have been washed white in His righteousness once and for all (Isaiah 61:10). When God looks at us now, He sees Christ's righteousness covering us. We belong to Him and are completely accepted, no matter what we do or how we perform.

4. What does God say about you, His precious child, in the following verses?

Romans 8:1

Isaiah 61:10

1 Peter 1:3-5

Isaiah 43:1-10

Psalm 103:10-12

4. Read Luke 15:11-24.

In verses 19 and 21, how does the son believe his position of worthiness has been affected by his sinful behavior?

In verses 22-24 what does his father communicate through his actions about the state of his son's worthiness?

The Prodigal son lost all his money and all his possessions as a result of his sin. He was carried away by the pleasure of his debauchery for a little while, but that was short-lived. It didn't take long for him to wake up alone, miserable and starving. The truth began to wash over him that his sin had deeply hurt not only himself but also the people he loved most.

When we sin as believers, God doesn't shield us from the consequences of our sins. Sin hurts us and hurts the ones we love. *But no sin we ever commit affects our worthiness in Jesus a single drop.* This is God's breathtaking grace at work. Our worthiness is untouchable because it is based completely on what Jesus did for us and not at all on what we do or don't do for Him. Even when we commit our ugliest sins as believers, even when we waste the precious gifts He gives us, the Father waits for us with loving and accepting arms.

The flip side of this is also true. When we follow God's path for our lives and obey Him with our whole hearts we reap the consequences of these choices. We unearth joy and fulfillment and satisfaction beyond our wildest dreams and He is able to use our lives in spectacular ways for His Kingdom. But our obedience and the good things we do can't make us *more* worthy, *more* acceptable or *more* pleasing in His eyes. It's already 100% finished. We are already *worthy in Jesus.*

Exploring Love and Belonging (pp. 24-28)

5. What is the difference between "belonging" and "fitting in"? In your life when have you felt the deepest sense of belonging? When have you felt like you were struggling to fit in? What caused these situations to feel so different?

6. How are "love" and "belonging" connected?

7. What is your first reaction when you hear the terms "self love" and "loving yourself?"

8. What is "self love" as described in this book? (See page 27.)

> "Let each of you look out not only for his own interests, but also for the interests of others."
> Philippians 2:4
>
> "…You shall love your neighbor as yourself." Matthew 22:39

9. Is the "self love" described in this book biblical?

Loving Others Well (pp. 28-30)

10. Do you think "self-love" and "self-acceptance" are prerequisites for loving others well? Do you think it's true we can only love and accept others as much as we love and accept ourselves? Explain.

The way we view and judge others is a mirror reflection of the way we view and judge ourselves, and how we view ourselves springs directly from our beliefs about how God views us!

Do we see Him as a drill sergeant, always demanding more and never satisfied? Or are we daily feeding on His abundant love and grace, believing that He is already completely satisfied with us because of Jesus?

The more we come boldly to His throne of grace and experience His love for us, the more we will be able to see ourselves through His eyes of love. And the more we see ourselves through His eyes the more we will see others in this light as well. His love consumes us and flows out from us to others.

11. What further light does 1 John 4:6-21 shed on this subject?

"The Things That Get in the Way"

Questions for Reflection & Discussion

Facing the Hard Things (pp. 31-38)

1. How do you think not talking about difficult topics like "shame, fear and vulnerability" keeps us from "living and loving with our whole hearts"? (See page 36.)

Gaining the Upper Hand On Shame (pp. 38-41)

2. What does fear have to do with shame? (See page 39.)

3. What is "shame resilience"? (See page 40.)

"The less we talk about shame, the more we have it. Shame needs three things to grow out of control in our lives: secrecy, silence & judgment. When something shaming happens and we keep it locked up, it festers and grows. It consumes us. We need to share our experience. Shame happens between people, and it heals between people…Shame loses power when it is spoken."—*The Gifts of Imperfection,* page 40

4. Sin and shame are close cousins. Read James 5:16. What happens when we confess our sins to another human being?

I have been a Christian for many years and confessing my sins to God usually isn't too difficult for me. I trust Him. I know He is a God of grace and that He will always forgive me.

Confessing my sins to other people, though—and not only my sins but also my "shame stories," sinful or not—for many years made me feel sick to my stomach. Literally. Talking about the hard things to God is relatively easy once we have an understanding of His unconditional love and grace, but speaking those stories out loud to another human being is an entirely different story.

Several years ago my husband Josh and I went through a painfully difficult period in our marriage. It all started when we moved to Asia together for the first time: Culture stress plus challenging jobs plus the fact that we were still newly married created a perfect storm that shook loose all kinds of baggage from our pasts neither of us had ever dealt with. Our hidden pain came hurdling out into the open aimed directly at each other. It was a dark time for both of us; we hurt one another deeply.

When we returned to America the next year we held high hopes that all our problems would disappear, but they didn't. Instead, they only seemed to intensify. It was then that God lit up James 5:16 for me as if with flashing fluorescent lights,

"Therefore, confess your sins to one another and pray for one another, that you may be healed." James 5:16a

I fought against and ignored this verse for a long time. I was doing all the other right things in my life; surely I would get better on my own. If I just read my Bible enough and prayed enough on my own God would heal me.

But He didn't. He stayed close to me and never left my side, but He didn't heal me. He wanted to heal me through other people, and reaching out to other people required a humility I didn't possess. He allowed more and more bitter pain to press down on me until finally I couldn't stand it any more. I knew I had to talk about it with other people no matter how much shame I felt and no matter how much doing so would hurt my pride.

For me putting James 5:16 into practice meant resolutely setting aside my pride and marching myself to a Christ-centered 12 step recovery meeting (Celebrate Recovery) at my church. I was so taken in and in awe of what I discovered there that I kept going back and going back. At Celebrate Recovery I saw James 5:16 being put into practice in the most beautiful way I had ever seen. It was a safe place for everyone to talk about their shame, struggles, sin and pain. It wasn't a place of judgment, it was a place of acceptance and love. We were all in it together.

It was there, as I slowly gained courage to talk more and more about my pain and my struggles *to other people*, that God finally began to heal me from the pain of my past; and not only me but my marriage too! It opened up a whole new dimension of freedom and joy in my life and a deeper relationship with Jesus as well. I am changed forever because of this experience. Now it is much easier for me to talk with others about new shame stories as they surface in my life.

James 5:16 is a tiny little verse but it reveals an incredibly powerful secret to anyone who is willing to listen. We blow right past it and ignore it because we don't *want* to hear it. We don't want to face this challenge. It is so much easier to keep everything hidden inside.

Don't let your pride keep you from experiencing the fullness of freedom and healing God desires to give you. It's not worth it. We Christians are forgiven—wonderfully, marvelously forgiven. But so many of us are broken and hurting. As long as we keep our shame and our sin hidden inside **we will not find healing**. We won't find true freedom from the sins that keep tripping us up. We won't experience freedom from the pain of our shame.

Sharing it—opening our deepest selves up to the light—makes healing possible. Emotional healing, spiritual healing, psychological healing—and in some cases even physical healing—can result from letting those shame stories out of the dungeon and into the light.

The Word doesn't say that we need to share our shame stories with the whole world. Sharing it with one person is often all that it takes, and it is wise and prudent to choose this person carefully.

We need to talk about our shame.

5. Have you ever seen or experienced the type of confession mentioned in James 5:16 being practiced among believers? What was it like?

6. For personal reflection only: Is there any hidden shame in your life that needs to be let out of the dungeon and brought into the light? Who is someone safe you could talk to about this shame?

Peeking Under the Rug of Shame (pp. 41-42)

7. Can you identify any shaming "self-talk" you sometimes think to yourself?

8. What part, if any, did "shaming" play in your family, school and/or church when you were growing up? Can you think of a time when you were shamed as a child?

9. What do shame and shaming look like in other cultures with which you might be familiar?

Discarding Old Shame Defenses (pp. 42-47)

10. On page 46 the author talks about three different ways people naturally attempt to handle shame. At different times we have probably all used all three of these different tactics. Can you identify which might be your default response?

11. What is one step you can take this week toward developing "shame resilience"?

GUIDEPOST #1

Questions for Reflection & Discussion

Exploring Authenticity (pp. 49-50)

> "Authenticity is the daily practice of letting go of who we think we're supposed to be and embracing who we are."—*The Gifts of Imperfection*, page 50

Practicing authenticity is about being real and genuine, not copied or fake. It's about allowing ourselves to be who we really are and embracing the unique person God has created us to be.

Practicing true authenticity requires *faith* and *humility*. To practice true authenticity we must exercise *faith* moment by moment by believing we are 100% worthy because of Jesus and special in His eyes, with a unique and important role to play in His Kingdom.

We must also choose *humility* by allowing our weaknesses and failures to be seen in the light, clinging to the truth that because of Jesus our weaknesses and failures and mistakes never disqualify us. We don't need to hide them. God wants to redeem them and shine through them for His glory.

1. Tell us about a person you know whom you would say practices authenticity. How have you seen authenticity exhibited in his or her life?

2. How does it make you feel to realize that being authentic isn't a one-time event, but a daily practice and choice?

The Courageous Nature of Authenticity (pp. 51-52)

3. In what ways does the world—media, society, culture or even the church—try to "make us everybody but ourselves"? (See page 51.)

4. Have you ever made a choice to practice authenticity and experienced "pushback" from family or friends as a result? (See page 51.) If yes, describe what happened. If no, what kinds of pushback do you think you might experience if you made a choice to practice authenticity in a new way?

5. Describe a time you took a risk and put your true self out there; a time when you shared an opinion or idea, did something new or that you hadn't yet mastered in front of others, or shared something you created. What happened when you took the risk?

Esther was a woman who chose to live her life with courageous authenticity.

In the Book of Esther, Ahasuerus, King of Persia, finds himself in the market for a new queen. He orders a search to be made throughout his entire kingdom for lovely young women who are chosen to participate in the beauty pageant of a lifetime. Word ripples throughout the land: the one woman who pleases the king will win his hand in marriage and the title Queen of Persia.

In chapter 2 we meet a godly, devoted, beautiful Jewish maiden named Esther who is among the girls chosen to present herself to the king.

6. Read Esther 2:12-17. How does Esther choose to practice authenticity in verses 13-15? What happens as a result?

"She was not solicitous, as the rest of the maidens were, to set herself off with artificial beauty; she required nothing but just what was appointed for her (Est. 2:15) and yet she was most acceptable…The king loved Esther above all the women." —Matthew Henry, *Matthew Henry's Commentary on the Whole Bible*

Each of the young women could choose whatever items she wanted from the women's quarters, adornments of all kinds: jewelry, fine clothing, who knows what other items. It would have been tempting to pile on the finery and doll herself up to try and impress the king, but Esther refrained. She went to him as herself. She didn't ask for anything from the women's quarters, she only wore what was suggested for her to wear. The king fell in love with her just the way she was.

In chapter 4 Esther faces an even more challenging opportunity to practice authenticity. Up to this point she has not revealed her full identity as a Jewess (see 2:10) because of the danger involved in doing so. However, God's people are being threatened and Esther is the only one in a position to help. Esther's Uncle Mordecai urges her to reveal her full, true identity and to plead for the King to protect her people.

7. Read Esther 3:5-4:17. Describe what is at stake in this story. What happens if Esther keeps silent? What does she risk if she speaks up and reveals her true identity?

God created each one of of us with a specific and unique role to play in His Kingdom. He chose us and called us for an important purpose. If we "remain silent" (pretending to be someone other than who we are, keeping our true personalities, dreams, gifts and ideas hidden), God is able to accomplish His purposes in another way, but we will *perish*. We will miss out on the full and abundant life that God has planned for us.

"For if you remain completely silent at this time, relief and deliverance will arise for the Jews from another place, but you and your father's house will perish. Yet who knows whether you have come to the kingdom for such a time as this?" Esther 4:14

What if He has chosen *you*—with your unique gifts and personality and background and passions and experiences and flaws and struggles—to be part of His kingdom for such a time as this?! He *has!*

8. What do we risk losing and missing if we choose to play it safe in our life and keep our true selves hidden?

9. What is one thing about yourself you sometimes hold back that you would like to begin sharing with the world?

10. What are some specific ways you think God might want to use you and your unique gifts for His kingdom?

When Authenticity Hurts (pp. 52-54)

Esther knew the risks of revealing her true identity. She put her whole *life* on the line. She was willing to take this risk because she believed it was worth it, that God had created her and placed her in her position in life for a reason.

Practicing authenticity is always a courageous act. Presenting our real selves to the world means taking a risk that we could be attacked, criticized or not liked. Painting a picture means there may be someone out there who doesn't want it hanging in their living room. Writing and publishing a book means it could get bad reviews on Amazon. Following our dreams means someone we love may disapprove. Wearing the styles we really like may mean we get snide comments from the fashion police. Expressing our passions means others may not share them. Sharing a belief or opinion means there are probably people who don't agree.

But *what if?* What if God wants to use these things to showcase His glory through us? Isn't that absolutely worth the risk?

Knowing that our worthiness isn't dependent on what other people think is what gives us the courage to be authentic. God's is the only opinion that matters and we already know His opinion of us: we are completely loved and accepted. We are *worthy in Jesus.*

11. What are some things we can do to care for ourselves if we put our real selves out there and get hurt in the process?

12. How could "making authenticity our number one goal when we go into a situation where we're feeling vulnerable" be a more helpful goal than the goals of "acceptance," "approval" or "being liked"? (See page 54.)

GUIDEPOST #2

Questions for Reflection & Discussion

Defining Perfectionism (pp. 55-57)

1. What is perfectionism?

2. How are shame and perfectionism linked?

Perfectionism is a cruel and unrelenting master. Night and day it dangles the tantalizing goal of perfection before our faces. We believe we can reach it. We work hard for it. We sacrifice all we have to get it.

But perfection always remains beyond our grasp.

For a large chunk of my life I took great pride in my perfectionism. I was absolutely trying to attain my own sense of worthiness through doing everything "perfectly." I knew, of course, that I'm actually not perfect and that I really can't do anything completely perfectly. But the closer I could get to that goal of perfection, the better, I believed. I couldn't let go.

It took suffering near-debilitating anxiety for me to finally recognize that my constant and compulsive straining toward the unobtainable illusion of perfection was doing nothing for me except causing pain for myself and for those I love.

Perfectionism is a trap, but the mistaken belief that perfectionism is a good thing is not uncommon.

Not long ago I shared with a friend of mine that I struggle with perfectionism and God has been helping me find more and more freedom from it. My friend looked confused and surprised. She told me she didn't agree that perfectionism is negative or unhealthy and maintained that Christians *should be* perfectionists, that we should be striving for perfection in everything we do. She quoted this verse: "Therefore you are to be perfect, as your heavenly Father is perfect." (Matthew 5:48 NASB)

3. Read Matthew 5:17-48. If you were in my shoes, how would you have responded to this friend?

In these verses Jesus goes out of His way to show us how impossible it is for us to reach God's perfect standards on our own.

In verse 20 He tells the people, "Unless your righteousness *exceeds* the righteousness of the scribes and Pharisees, you will by no means enter the kingdom of heaven."

Think about the scribes and Pharisees. Jesus speaks with them often throughout His ministry. These guys were ultimate spiritual perfectionists. They were the best of the best, spiritually speaking, fully committed to doing everything they could to follow the Law to the letter.

But even the best efforts of the scribes and Pharisees weren't good enough. Jesus says, in effect, *You thought you were doing a pretty good job of following the Law? Let me blow that illusion right out of the water. You are not even close to my standard. You think you're doing a good thing by not murdering, but I tell you if you are angry with your brother without cause you are in danger of judgment. If you say 'You fool!' you shall be in danger of hell fire.* (See 5:21, 22.)

Ouch!

If you get to verse 48 in this passage ("you are to be perfect, as your heavenly Father is perfect") and feel a sense of desperation and fear because you know you can't do it, you are responding exactly how Jesus wants you to respond when you get to this verse.

It is impossible for us broken human beings to produce anything that is perfect. Attaining perfection, for a human being, is only an illusion. Perfection is something only God can ever attain.

Jesus highlights this for us in Matthew 5 *to show us our desperate need for Him.*

The only way we can impress and please God is by understanding that we are not impressing Him one bit by any of our good actions or by our striving for perfection.

He doesn't want us straining for His approval. He wants us resting in the approval which was 100% won for us by our Champion Jesus Christ.

"*You are already clean* because of the word which I have spoken to you. Abide in Me, and I in you. As the branch cannot bear fruit of itself unless it abides in the vine, so neither can you unless you abide in Me. I am the vine, you are the branches; he who abides in Me and I in him bears much fruit; for apart from Me you can do nothing." John 15:3-5

When we strive to gain the approval of God and of other people through perfectionism we are trying to find our worthiness in ourselves. We are wasting our time and wasting precious energy, because our worthiness isn't found there. We are already worthy because of Jesus.

"Are you so foolish? Having begun in the Spirit are you now being made perfect in the flesh?" Galatians 3:3

Dear friends, let that project go. You have checked it over sufficiently, you don't need to hover over it for the 100th time looking for errors. If there are any mistakes left in it, *you are still worthy.*

Serve that chocolate cake that is a little gooey in the center. Serve it without apology and with great love. You are not a perfect cook but *you are beautifully worthy.*

Play the song with your whole heart even though you still stumble through that one bar. You will never be a perfect musician, but *you are absolutely worthy.*

Let your grass grow for a few more days! Finish reading that novel you're so enjoying instead. Let your neighbors gossip about your scraggly lawn. Neither the height of your grass nor your neighbors' opinion of you defines your worthiness. *You are worthy in Jesus.*

4. Read Colossians 2:9-3:4. What do we learn in these verses about the completeness we have in Christ? What has happened to all the requirements God had for us?

5. What is the difference between "perfectionism" and "healthy achieving"? (See page 56, 57.)

Overcoming Perfectionism (pp. 57-60)

6. Where do you think you fall on the "perfectionism continuum"? (See pages 57, 58.) Think about the way you approach your work, hobbies, home life, school, family time, etc. Where does perfectionism show up in your life and to what extent does it affect your life?

7. What does the author mean by "fake it till you make it" on page 58?

8. What are the three elements of "self compassion" that can help us combat perfectionism? (See pages 59, 60.) Paraphrase the description of each element.

9. Which of these three aspects of self compassion is hardest for you to practice?

Understanding How Our Perfectionism Harms Others (pp. 60-61)

10. How do perfectionism and lack of self-compassion ultimately lead to judgment of others?

11. Think of three areas in which you are quick to judge others.

12. Can you trace these back to any perfectionism or lack of self-compassion in these same three areas toward yourself?

Embracing Our Imperfections (pp. 61-62)

> "There is a crack in everything. That's how the light gets in." —Leonard Cohen, as quoted in *The Gifts of Imperfection*, page 61

13. How can God use our "cracks"—that is, our mistakes, our weaknesses and our imperfections—for His glory?

GUIDEPOST #3

Questions for Reflection & Discussion

Displaying Resilience in Trials (pp. 63-65)

1. What is resilience?

2. What are the 5 most common factors of resilient people? (See page 64.)

Holding Fast to Hope (pp. 65-67)

3. In the first part of this chapter, how does the author define "hope"?

4. Biblical hope looks a little different and goes much deeper than this. How would you define or describe the hope that carries believers through difficult times? What is a favorite verse that speaks of this hope?

Apprehending False Voices (pp. 67-69)

> "Practicing critical awareness is about reality-checking the messages and expectations that drive the 'never good enough' gremlins."—*The Gifts of Imperfection*, page 67
>
> "Finally, brethren, whatever is true, whatever is honorable, whatever is right, whatever is pure, whatever is lovely, whatever is of good repute, if there is any excellence and if anything worthy of praise, dwell on these things." Philippians 4:8

5. What are some examples of false messages that slip into your mind when you're reading magazines; watching television; talking with family members, friends or coworkers; even attending church? What false messages have become automatic thoughts that pop up in your brain all on their own?

6. What practical things can we do to increase our awareness of false voices in our lives?

Feeling Our Feelings (pp. 69-73)

For so many of us, talking about our feelings is strange and uncomfortable. For others it is downright terrifying.

Some of us brush it aside, "Oh, I'm not a very emotional person." Some of us think it doesn't apply to us, "I'm a guy, guys aren't emotional," or my old standby, "I'm from New England…New Englanders are stoics."

Author Lynn Hoffman writes about feelings in this way:

> Feelings, what are they? Feelings are our body's response to our belief that our needs are not being met. We were created by God, in His image. We were gifted with the capacity to love as well as the ability to feel joy and passion. These positive emotions produce warm, pleasant feelings that cause us to smile, laugh, dance and live life abundantly.
>
> We have also been created with what might be described as "negative emotions." They include anger, pain, fear, shame and guilt. While these emotions can be distressing, they exist to let us know that something is wrong, may need our attention, or may need to change. You can consider these to be similar to the warning lights on the dashboard of our car.
>
> Unfortunately, many of us were taught that it was not okay to have any emotions or feelings. Often our feelings were met with discipline or rejection. Or we were told that what we felt didn't matter. Many of us learned to survive by denying or stuffing our feelings, limiting our expression of our feelings, or learning to express only positive feelings to stay safe.
>
> Consequently, many of us have no idea how we feel. This is not uncommon. (*Steps Into God's Grace*, pages 5, 6)

I was one of those who for many years had no idea what I was feeling. I didn't cry much, I didn't get angry often, I didn't really react in a visible way even when I was happy or sad. I just assumed I wasn't a very emotional person.

But I was mistaken. It wasn't that I'm not an emotional person—I am! (I believe we all are!) I was just an expert stuffer. I didn't always feel safe to express my emotions—and I didn't know how—so I stuffed them deep down inside.

It wasn't until my husband and I hit the road bumps in our marriage that it started becoming evident that something was way off with the way I had been handling my feelings. The stuffed feelings from all those years started leaking out in all the wrong directions. I had no idea what to do with them.

Over time and with the help of some wonderful friends and a gifted counselor I began to learn what a gift feelings actually are, and what a relief it is to recognize and feel and express them in a healthy way.

It seems like feeling our feelings should be natural but I had to learn from scratch. Here's my go-to guide for feeling my feelings:

FEELING MY FEELINGS

1. *Slow down.* As soon as you become aware of some feeling that needs attention, slow down instead of speeding up!

2. *Identify* the feeling or feelings. Sad? Afraid? Disappointed? Angry? Joyful?

3. *Accept* the feeling.

4. *Express* the feeling. Say it out loud, to God, in a journal.

5. *Feel* the feeling. Be still. Don't shrink from it or push it away. Let the feeling wash over you. Remain in it until it naturally starts to subside. Cry if you need to cry, punch a pillow if you need to punch a pillow.

6. *Ask:* What is this feeling telling you? Is there some way you need to care for yourself? (For example: Is there someone you need to talk to in order to resolve a conflict? Do you need to rest or take time for yourself?)

7. Are any feelings "sinful" or "wrong"?

8. See pages 68-70. What do you sometimes use to "numb" or "take the edge off" difficult emotions that leave you feeling vulnerable and uncertain?

9. Are you able to identify and feel and express your way through painful emotions or do you more often try to push them away?

10. This week, carve out a little extra time for your feelings. Try out my handy guide for feeling feelings when you feel one rising up. Write about your experience here:

11. How is JOY just as "thorny and sharp as any of the dark emotions"? (See page 73.)

Maintaining Perspective in Hard Times (pp. 74-75)

12. At the end of this chapter the author shares how spirituality can give purpose, meaning and perspective to our lives in difficult times. Those of us who know and love Jesus have access to true purpose, meaning and perspective. What purpose, meaning or perspective have you discovered in the Lord when you when you have experienced suffering in the past?

13. Our connection with God and our ability to experience His presence right here with us is hands-down what helps the most when we're in the middle of painful situations. What verses remind you of the truth that you are not alone—not in the most traumatic moments of your life nor in your everyday stresses and anxieties?

GUIDEPOST #4

Questions for Reflection & Discussion

Introducing Joy & Gratitude (pp. 77-78)

1. How would you define or describe biblical joy?

2. Think about your life. How have you seen joy and gratitude linked? What are some of your favorite Bible verses that speak of joy and/or gratitude?

Practicing Gratitude (pp. 78-79)

3. What does "practicing gratitude" currently look like in your life?

4. What is one new thing you could try or change to build more intentional gratitude into your everyday life?

Savoring Joy (pp. 79-82)

5. What is the difference between happiness and joy?

"And your heart shall swell with joy." Isaiah 60:5b

6. Think of a time when you were aware of experiencing joy. What did it feel like? What prompted the experience?

"Twinkle lights are the perfect metaphor for joy. Joy is not a constant. It comes to us in moments—often ordinary moments. Sometimes we miss out on the bursts of joy because we're too busy chasing down extraordinary moments. Other times we're so afraid of the dark that we don't dare let ourselves enjoy the light."—*The Gifts of Imperfection*, pages 80, 81

7. What are some ordinary moments that have stirred joy in your heart?

"Most of us have experienced being on the edge of joy only to be overcome by vulnerability and thrown into fear."—*The Gifts of Imperfection*, page 82

8. Can you think of a time when this happened to you? Describe it.

Believing It's Enough (pp. 82-85)

9. How much do you buy into the "myth of scarcity"? (See page 82.) That is, how often do you find yourself thinking there isn't enough time, isn't enough energy, isn't enough sleep, etc. Not enough_____.?

In our culture this myth is *so* prevalent. And it really is a myth. It's more than a myth: it is a deceptive lie that has come straight from the mouth of our Enemy.

Think about it. Was God playing a mean trick on us when He created Day with 24 hours in it?

Was He secretly thinking, "Hahaha, I'm only going to give them 24 hours. I know it's not going to be even close to enough time for them. I want to see them running around like crazy trying to finish everything I want them to do. I want to see them busy and stressed all their days."?

No way. That is not our God.

He gave us 24 hours and then He said it was GOOD.

It is *enough*.

Maybe we don't have enough time for what we are currently *trying* to accomplish. Maybe we don't have enough resources for what we think we're *supposed to* accomplish. Maybe we don't have enough energy for what we *plan* to accomplish tomorrow, or next week, or next month.

But we absolutely have enough time and energy and resources for what GOD desires to accomplish through us *today*.

I now recognize the thought "There's not enough!" as a big flashing red warning light.

If there's not enough time or energy or resources for what I have on my plate I need to make a hard stop and take a really good look at that plate.

What is on my plate that God didn't put there?

If there was ever an important person with loads of people to help and important work to be done—a whole world to be saved!—it was Jesus Christ. He was constantly surrounded by crowds of needy people. He knew the needs of this world more deeply than we ever will.

But think back through the Gospels. Jesus was never in danger of not having enough time or resources to accomplish what He had been placed on the earth to accomplish. He was never in a hurry. There is not one single verse that tells us He hustled or scrambled or put the disciples into high-powered hurry-up-and-get-it-done mode.

Jesus was purposeful, but peaceful. Passionate, but unhurried. Aware of the vastness of His mission, but absolutely present in each moment of each day. Compassionate for the needs of multitudes, but zeroed in on the one person standing in front of Him.

We do well to walk in His footsteps.

We do well to walk slowly.

There is only as much to do as I can do peacefully today.

10. Do you have too much on your plate right now? What may be on there that God hasn't put there?

11. How could believing the "myth of scarcity" be stealing our joy?

12. Read Exodus 16. What does this story teach us about God's provision for His people and about the "myth of scarcity"?

> "Joy is what happens to us when we allow ourselves to recognize how good things really are."—Marianne Williamson, as quoted in *The Gifts of Imperfection*, page 84

13. What are you grateful for this week?

GUIDEPOST #5

Questions for Reflection & Discussion

Trusting Your Gut (pp. 87-89)

1. According to the author, what is "intuition" or "trusting your gut"? (See pages 87-89.)

I love that the author strips away the mystical, wizardly mist that sometimes surrounds the topic of "intuition." Intuition is not a shot in the dark, it's not something that happens when we rub a Magic 8 Ball. Intuition is a special way God has designed our brains to process information and come to conclusions. We can treat this specific kind of decision-making process the same as we do any other.

Is our intuition 100% right all the time? Of course not!

"The heart is deceitful above all things, and desperately wicked; who can know it?" Jeremiah 17:9

As Christians we never rely completely on ourselves and our own ability to measure a situation rightly.

"'For My thoughts are not your thoughts, Nor are your ways My ways,' says the Lord. 'For as the heavens are higher than the earth, So are My ways higher than your ways, And My thoughts than your thoughts.'" Isaiah 55:8, 9

"Trust in the Lord with all your heart, And lean not on your own understanding; In all your ways acknowledge Him, and He shall direct your paths." Proverbs 3:5, 6

And yet God has designed our brains to think and consider and make decisions in a wonderful, marvelous way. Many people are gifted very strongly with this intuitive brain function. We can learn to wield it with confidence!

Something miraculous happens to us when we become believers. The Bible says that we *have the mind of Christ!* (See I Corinthians 2:16.) Isn't that breathtaking? The very mind of Christ!

As we seek Him, feast on His Word, grow in Him and abide in Him, we learn to tap into His mind more and more. He fills our minds with His wisdom which seeps right into our thinking and decision-making processes. Over time we are able to discern more and more quickly and confidently His guidance in our life.

"Get wisdom! Get understanding! Do not forget, nor turn away from the words of my mouth. Do not forsake her, and she will preserve you; Love her, and she will keep you." Proverbs 4:5, 6

"But he who is spiritual judges all things, yet he himself is rightly judged by no one. For 'who has known the mind of the Lord that he may instruct Him?' *But we have the mind of Christ.*" I Corinthians 2:15, 16

"And do not be conformed to this world, but be transformed by the renewing of your mind, that you may prove what is that good and acceptable and perfect will of God." Romans 12:2

In my life, the underlying obstacle that causes me to doubt my own instincts and the Holy Spirit's leading in my heart is this: straight up *fear.*

Fear of hearing it all wrong, fear of making a mistake, fear of making a complete fool of myself.

My own insecurity and unbelief in my worthiness rear up and I'm terrified of the shame I'll feel if I make a poor decision. When I dig down deep I find I'm scared I'll be disqualified from my worthiness.

As we all know by now, this is nothing but a big fat lie. It can't happen.

When we are trusting in God and acknowledging Him in all our ways; when we are growing in Him and relying on His Word; when we are yielding our minds and hearts to Him, we can trust His mind at work in us. We can trust Him working through our intuition.

We can act on our gut with confidence, knowing that even if we do make a mistake, which we are bound to do from time to time as humans, *we are 100% worthy in Jesus!*

2. Would you say you are an intuitive person? Why or why not? Can you describe the way your intuition works?

3. When is it hardest for you to act on what your "gut" is telling you?

4. When we have a decision to make and and find ourselves "polling" others for their opinions (see page 88), what might that tell us about ourselves and our situation?

5. As you have grown in the Lord, how have you noticed God teaching you wisdom and changing the way you think?

Walking By Faith (pp. 90-91)

6. What is the author's definition of faith? (See page 90.) How does that measure up to the definition we find in Hebrews 11:1?

7. When do you find it hardest to exercise faith? How does your desire for certainty play a role in this?

8. What is one circumstance in your life right now that is challenging you to "walk by faith, not by sight"? (See 2 Corinthians 5:7.)

9. What have you found helps you to keep believing and keep walking forward when fear of uncertainty threatens your faith?

10. Spend some time meditating on Hebrews 11 & 12. What is God speaking to your heart about faith through this passage?

GUIDEPOST #6

Questions for Reflection & Discussion

Understanding Our Tendency to Compare (pp. 93-95)

> "Comparison is all about conformity and competition…When we compare, we want to be the best or have the best of our group… It's not cultivate self-acceptance, belonging and authenticity; it's be just like everyone else, only better."—*The Gifts of Imperfection*, page 94

1. If you are honest, how much time and energy do you spend comparing yourself with others?

(How you look, how you cook, what you own, how you keep your house, how you parent, how you spend your time, how you minister to others, how you dress, what you eat, how you pray, how your children behave, how you spend your money, how you Quiet Time, your marriage, your spouse, your calling, your garden, your car, your relationship with God—the list of possibilities for comparison is infinite!)

The first time I read this chapter in *The Gifts of Imperfection* I didn't stop to think much about it because initially I didn't think I had a problem with comparing. At least I was pretty sure I didn't have as much of a problem with it as some other people do. (!)

The more I slowed down to listen to my thoughts, however, the more I realized I compare myself with others far more often than I would like to admit.

Like daily.

Many times a day.

When my kids are the best-behaved children in the room I of course notice this and unconsciously give myself a little pat on the back. My ego gets a nice gratifying puff of clear air.

But when mine are the rascals and the ones throwing the tantrums (a much more common occurrence of late) I feel deflated and like I have lost value somehow. I immediately begin scanning for something else to give me that little boost of worth. "Well my kids didn't sleep well last night. If they had slept better they would be little angels right now." Or… "At least my kids are better dressed, or smarter, or more independent…"

It's ridiculous, isn't it? Seriously. It makes me sick when I see those kinds of thoughts in black and white. It's absolutely disgusting.

Why do we do it?

This is what I have discovered: Comparison is tied to our insecurity and at its very core has everything to do with *pride.*

"Pride gets no pleasure out of having something, only out of having more of it than the next person." —C.S. Lewis, *Mere Christianity*

Comparing is not just some distant relative of pride; comparing is in itself an act of pure pride.

Timothy Keller writes, "Spiritual pride is the illusion that we are competent to run our own lives, achieve our own sense of self-worth and find a purpose big enough to give us meaning in life without God." (*The Freedom of Self-Forgetfulness)**

When we compare, we're eager to find ways in which we are better than other people. We scramble to find something—anything ("My bathroom faucet is so much nicer than this lady's!")— to hold onto which will give us even the slightest positive feeling of value and importance. We are straining to buoy up our own faulty sense of worthiness rather than resting in and glorying in the true worthiness that Christ has already won for us.

2. What can we learn about comparing from the following verses? (Choose two if you don't have time to look at them all.)

Mathew 7:1-5

Matthew 20:1-16

Mark 9:33-37

Luke 10:38-42

John 21:15-23

Romans 14:1-13

2 Corinthians 10

James 5:9

"Comparison is the thief of happiness." —Laura Williams, as quoted in *The Gifts of Imperfection*, page 95

3. In what ways is comparing robbing you of joy?

Most—in fact, I'm pretty sure *all*—of us, if we are honest, have made a painful habit out of comparing. Without a conscious awareness of our worthiness in Jesus we do it naturally, without even realizing it. Comparing ourselves with others becomes an automatic thought process of our brains.

Thankfully for us all, this habit and automatic thought process can be changed. With God's help we can absolutely retrain our brains and learn to live out of our worthiness in Jesus without needing to compare. We can learn to enjoy the successes and joys of others without feeling even the slightest twinge of a threat to our egos.

Sounds amazing, doesn't it? How do we do it?

Our road to victory over comparing is, I believe, three-fold:

1. *Capture each ugly, comparing thought as it comes.*

As soon as we become aware that we are comparing, we can stop the thought in its tracks.

"Casting down arguments and every high thing that exalts itself against the knowledge of God, bringing every thought into captivity to the obedience of Christ…" 2 Corinthians 10:5

2. *Confess it to God for what it is:* sin.

"For we dare not class ourselves or compare ourselves with those who commend themselves. But they, measuring themselves by themselves, and comparing themselves among themselves, are not wise." 2 Corinthians 10:12

3. *Replace it with Truth.*

Replace it with the truth that we are 100% worthy and accepted and approved. We are enough, no matter how we measure up to other people (or even to our own standards for ourselves!), because of the work and Word of our Lord Jesus Christ.

"But 'He who glories, let him glory in the Lord.' For not he who commends himself is approved, but whom the Lord commends." 2 Corinthians 10:17,18

The more we capture our comparing thoughts and replace them with truth, the more we will learn to live purely out of our worthiness in Jesus!

4. What can you do this week to heighten your awareness of your thoughts—specifically your propensity to compare? (Perhaps setting some sort of reminder throughout the day, starting a thought journal, sharing your new realizations about your thoughts daily with a family member or friend...)

Unleashing Our Creativity (pp. 95-97)

5. Do you see yourself as a creative person? Why or why not?

6. Do you or have you ever maintained a negative attitude about creativity similar to what the author describes on page 95? Why or why not?

7. How might doubting our worthiness in Jesus keep us from spending more time in creative endeavors?

8. What are some of the joys and benefits that come from creating?

9. How is expressing creativity encouraged and/or modeled in the Bible?

10. How do you enjoy using the creativity God has given you?

11. What is one creative thing you love doing that you might like to do more often? What is one new expression of creativity you would like to try?

*Recommended Reading: *The Freedom of Self-Forgetfulness* by Timothy Keller

GUIDEPOST #7

Questions for Reflection & Discussion

The Lost Art of Play (pp. 99-101)

1. Describe the last time you played.

2. What do you think keeps you from playing more?

3. What are the benefits of play? How have you experienced these benefits in your life?

4. List several ideas of playful things you could do by yourself, with your family, or with friends.

5. Have you been holding onto "exhaustion as a status symbol and productivity as self-worth?" (See page 102.)

6. How was rest and play viewed in your family when you were growing up?

A Theology of Rest (pp. 101-104)

7. Does "rest-filled" or "stress-filled" more accurately describe the current state of your life?

8. What blocks you from making more intentional time for physical, spiritual and emotional rest?

9. What activities/non-activities are most restful to you?

10. How is taking time for play and rest counter-cultural?

"Come to Me, all you who labor and are heavy laden, and I will give you rest. Take My yoke upon you and learn from Me, for I am gentle and lowly in heart, and you will find rest for your souls. For My yoke is easy and My burden is light." Matthew 11:28-30

Jesus is beckoning us even now. Do you hear Him? The straining, the striving, the pushing, the overloading of our bodies, our brains and our hearts…

It can stop.

Now.

Come.

Come to Me!

Come, my tired child. You are tired from trying to hold it all together. You are exhausted from your fear of failing. You are burdened with an ever-gnawing worry that you're not enough, that you need to do more. That you need to prove yourself to the world and to me Me.

Just come.

I will give you rest.

We may think that pushing ourselves past our limitations and overworking for the cause of Christ and for the sake of our families is the path of godliness, but we have been deceived.

So many of us carry this burden, but it has never been the load He asks us to bear.

Rest is never an afterthought with God. He takes rest very, very seriously.

In the very first pages of Scripture—even before He creates man and woman—God introduces the concept of rest to the universe. Deliberate, intentional, regular rest has always and forever been an important, critical, beautiful part of His plan for us.

"And He rested on the seventh day from all His work which He had done." Genesis 2:2b

We all already know God wasn't tired. We know no work is difficult for God, not even that of creating the entire universe. He wasn't fatigued, He wasn't at the end of His rope, He wasn't burnt out.

And yet He rested.

If God rested after His work when He didn't even need to, why are we people—whom God created with limitations: physical, spiritual, and emotional limitations—so afraid of rest? Why are we acting as if we are God and don't need rest?

God rested to give us an example, absolutely…to set a precedent from the beginning of time for all the world and for all mankind. He knew we needed that example to follow because our bodies were created to function with regular, plentiful rest even as they were created to need daily water. Rest is part of the rhythm of life.

But there is more.

God rested not just to give us an example but also simply because He is the God of rest.

The God of rest.

There is no other god in the history of the religions of the world that can boast such an attribute. What other god offers his followers *rest*?

Rest is part of who God is. It is part of what He does. Rest is in His very nature.

"My presence will go with you, and I will give you rest." Exodus 33:14

Wherever God's presence is realized, there is rest.

Our tiredness, our very weakness, is a beautiful treasure. It is a gift God has given us to remind us we are His creatures, we are limited, and we are dependent on Him. Our tiredness leads us to His arms of rest.

Rest requires faith because the rest God calls us to is absolutely counter-cultural. The rest He calls us to is revolutionary and goes against "the wisdom of this world."

"Six days shall you work, but on the seventh day you shall rest; *in plowing time and harvest you shall rest.*" Exodus 34:21

Did you hear that? God says, *I want you to observe the holiness of rest always. I know when your work gets busy—when you're in the groove of plowing, when the harvest is ripe and falling off the vine and there's pressure to get it all in—I know you are going to be tempted to push through and forgo rest.*

Don't do it. Don't do it. Trust Me, and rest.

Resting—ceasing from our work and from our ministry—even when there's more to be done, even in the midst of the busiest seasons of our lives, takes great discipline, great strength of character and great *faith*.

Intentional, holy rest so bold that it takes a day off right in the middle of harvest shows God we trust Him. Resting shows a watching world that He is the One who provides for us and we depend on Him. When we rest, we display one of God's highest and most holy characteristics. When we rest, we honor God.

The Enemy loves to whisper in the ears of God's chosen ones, "Work, work, work! Harder, harder, harder! Push! Achieve! You cannot afford to slow down!"

We ignore our body's physical signs which scream for us to stop and lie down or go see a doctor. We ignore our emotional red flags which warn us to slow down to care for our hearts and relationships. We ignore the spiritual slumps which signal we're running on empty.

When we refuse to rest we refuse to accept our rightful place as limited beings who are dependent on an all-powerful God. When we refuse to rest, we defy Him in pride. We shout to Him that we can do it, that we can do something worthwhile without His help.

It's not what God intends for us, dear friends. He says,

"In returning and rest you shall be saved; In quietness and confidence shall be your strength." Isaiah 30:15

"And He said to them, 'Come aside by yourselves to a deserted place and rest a while.' For there were many coming and going, and they did not even have time to eat." Mark 6:31

We can let go of the irrational fear that keeps us grinding on and pushing through our weariness...the fear that if we choose to rest our work will come to a grinding halt, that our lives won't amount to anything worthwhile, that *we won't be worthy.*

We are worthy in Jesus!

Resting isn't the end of what God wants to accomplish in and through us, it's just the beginning. *Our greatest work requires our greatest rest.*

11. Read Hebrews 4:4-13. There is rest waiting for you in heaven. Have you entered the rest that is waiting for you here today?

GUIDEPOST #8

Questions for Reflection & Discussion

Radiating Calm (pp. 105-107)

> "Anxiety is extremely contagious, but so is calm." —Harriet Lerner, as quoted in *The Gifts of Imperfection*, page 106

1. Think of someone you know whose presence spreads calm and peace. What is calming about this person? Can you describe it? If you are able, give them a call or shoot them an email and ask them the secret to their calm and peace-filled life.

2. When you walk into a room do you more often diffuse calm or leak anxiety? (If you are unsure or want a second opinion ask an honest family member or friend!)

3. Take a look at the verses listed below. How did Jesus exhibit calm, peace and presence, even in the midst of incredibly stressful situations? (If you don't have time to read them all, pick two.)

Mark 4:35-41

Luke 8:41-50

John 8:1-11

John 11:1-16

Luke 23:1-9, 27-34

4. What clues do the following verses give us about the source of Jesus' unprecedented example of calm and peace?

Matthew 6:34

Matthew 14:23

Mark 1:35

John 14:10

John 14:26-27

5. What everyday practices help you maintain calm?

Entering the Stillness (pp. 107-110)

6. What is the difference between calm and stillness?

"Then He said, 'Go out, and stand on the mountain before the Lord.' And behold, the Lord passed by, and a great and strong wind tore into the mountains and broke the rocks in pieces before the Lord, but the Lord was not in the wind; and after the wind an earthquake, but the Lord was not in the earthquake; and after the earthquake a fire, but the Lord was not in the fire; and after the fire *a still small voice.*" I Kings 19:11, 12

"Practicing stillness" is tucked quietly back here in the middle of Guidepost #8, but this age-old practice and art remains one of the most beautiful, powerful—and perhaps least discovered—secrets of the Spirit-drenched Christian life.

Stillness in the presence of God is a quiet, hidden little path that few ever pause to explore. Those who do find that it leads directly to the bubbling brook of His vibrant life and power and presence and peace, able to soak and satisfy our hearts unlike anything else in all the world.

It takes intentionality and practice to learn how to separate ourselves from the noise of the world and to quiet the multitudes of thoughts and voices buzzing in our heads. But as we return to the well again and again, waiting quietly at His feet, it becomes easier and easier to enter into the stillness where He is found. Oh the joys and delights that are waiting for us there!

"Surely I have calmed and quieted my soul, Like a weaned child with his mother; Like a weaned child is my soul within me." Psalm 131:2

"My soul, wait in silence for God only, For my hope is from Him." Psalm 62:5 (NASB)

In my own life it was as I learned to listen to God more in the stillness—and talk less—that my prayer life and personal relationship with God began to soar like a kite in the wind. In the silence I find the deep, satisfying and vibrant relationship with the Living God I always longed for.

Being still requires a firm belief in our worthiness in Jesus. Without it we remain agitated and busy in our prayers. When our belief in our worthiness in Jesus is shaky we unconsciously make an effort to impress or please God or to live up to our own expectations of what prayer is supposed to look like. We try to pray for all the right things and focus on making it all the way to the bottom of our prayer lists.

When we believe that we are 100% worthy in Jesus, though, and are able to rest in that, we can finally be still. This opens the door for our prayer times to become a beautiful two-way conversation between us and our God. He speaks to us and He guides us—even in our prayers back to Him!

God is alive. He is waiting and longing to speak to us, touch us and fill each and every one of us in a special and personal way…if only we will come and be still. If only we will stop long enough to kneel and listen for His voice which whispers deep inside our hearts.

"No longer did I need to work so hard to think, pray, or trust, because the Holy Spirit's 'gentle whisper' in my heart was God's prayer in the secret places of my soul. It was His answer to all my questions, and His life and strength for my soul and body…This is precisely how our spirit drinks in the life of our risen Lord. And then we are enabled to face life's conflicts and responsibilities, like a flower that has absorbed the cool and refreshing drops of dew throughout the darkness of night. Yet just as dew never falls on a stormy night, the dew of His grace never covers a restless soul." —A.B. Simpson (as quoted in *Streams in the Desert*, June 30)

7. Up until now, to what extent has practicing stillness been a part of your daily life and walk with God?

8. What are the biggest obstacles you face when it comes to practicing stillness?

9. What motivates you to spend time with God? Do you believe that you are 100% accepted by God because of Jesus, that He is always waiting for you with open arms and a loving smile? Or do you more often feel pressure to please Him and perform for Him?

"For we do not have a High Priest who cannot sympathize with our weaknesses, but was in all points tempted as we are, yet without sin. Let us therefore come boldly to the throne of grace, that we may obtain mercy and find grace to help in time of need." Hebrews 4:15, 16

10. This week, set aside a special time to be still before the Lord. Come believing in your worthiness and ask Him to help you find stillness in His presence. Quiet your heart and mind and listen. Listen for His gentle whisper. Some people find it helpful to go into a quiet room and close the door, to kneel down on the floor, to light a candle, or to go outside into nature.

As you quiet your heart and mind, meditate on Psalm 46:10:

"Be still, and know that I am God;
I will be exalted among the nations,
I will be exalted in the earth!"

Journal about your experience here:

GUIDEPOST #9

Questions for Reflection & Discussion

Finding Our Purpose (pp. 111-113)

> "Perhaps you are unaware of the fact that you are the customized expression of a loving God. You been endowed with unique mix of competencies and the desire and drive to use them in pursuit of an outcome of unrivaled personal importance. Your life has meaning built into it. Effectively, you have an exciting, challenging, and achievable destiny if you will but discover and embrace who you are designed to be."—Arthur F. Miller, Jr. with Howard D. Hendricks, *The Power of Uniqueness*

The life journey of the Christian who is actively pursuing God's heart is more exciting and more fulfilling than any other journey on earth. He bestows on us the high privilege of knowing, intimately, the God of the universe, and He offers us the opportunity to discover and become the truest version of the special person He created us to be. If we allow Him to, He will bring to fruition the fullness of the specific, uniquely tailored purpose for which He has placed us here on this earth. What could ever be more fulfilling than that?

"The generic meaning of *sanctification* is 'the state of proper functioning.' To sanctify someone or something is to set that person or thing apart for the use intended by its designer. A pen is 'sanctified' when used to write. Eyeglasses are 'sanctified' when used to improve sight. In the theological sense, things are sanctified when they are used for the purpose God intends. A human being is sanctified, therefore, when he or she lives according to God's design and purpose." (*Baker's Evangelical Dictionary of Theology*)

Each of us was born with a special set of innate talents and strengths. In the beginning of our lives, and in our walks with Christ, those strengths and gifts are rough and clumsy. Many of us are confused about what our strengths and gifts are. Some of us know what they are but are using them for our own purposes rather than God's.

As we walk forward in Christ, continuously seeking His face, God undertakes His breathtaking work of sanctification in us. He begins to bring our gifts to the surface. Slowly but surely He strips us and frees us from false pretenses and the baggage that keeps us from using our gifts. He guides us to the right locations at key moments in our lives so that our talents can be used to their true and full intended design.

God is deeply committed and invested in helping us find and develop our strengths and talents. He has given them to us to *use* so that His glory can shine through us and our work!

"For we are God's handiwork, created in Christ Jesus to do good works, which God prepared in advance for us to do." Ephesians 2:10 (NIV)

God will not hesitate to set us in whatever circumstances necessary, difficult and ideal, to hone and sharpen our gifts. He will stand back and allow us stumble and fail until will see clearly what our strengths are *not*. He will take great care to teach us that our strengths are worthless for His Kingdom when separated from Him and His might. Sometimes He lets us wander in uncertainty and darkness for long stretches at a time so that when He finally shines His light on His path and design for us He will get all the glory.

Over time, who we are and all the work we do, professionally or unprofessionally, reflects His glory more and more and more.

"But let patience have its perfect work, that you may be perfect and complete, lacking nothing." James 1:4

"By this My Father is glorified, that you bear much fruit; so you will be My disciples." John 15:8

Solomon, the wisest man who ever lived, said this about finding meaningful work:

"Here is what I have seen: It is good and fitting for one to eat and drink, and to enjoy the good of all his labor in which he toils under the sun all the days of his life which God gives him; for it is his heritage. As for every man to whom God has given riches and wealth, and given him power to eat of it, to receive his heritage and rejoice in his labor— this is the gift of God. For he will not dwell unduly on the days of his life, because God keeps him busy with the joy of his heart." Ecclesiastes 5:18-20

Our work and the fruit of our labor is our heritage. Rejoicing in our labor is a gift from God! God wants to keep us busy all our days with the joy of our heart: the meaningful work He has prepared for us.

I know from experience this verse doesn't make any sense to those of us dreamers who are, for the time being, stuck in the brown cubicle of a tall office building organizing files and sipping subpar coffee from a styrofoam cup.

When God called my husband Josh to seminary He called me away from a dream position in Asia where I was discipling young women on fire for Jesus to a lonely office cubicle in Dallas, TX. Someone had to earn money to pay for food and tuition fees and that someone was me. I did it willingly, but my gifts of writing and designing and shepherding were seemingly put on the shelf for several years.

During those years I often felt guilty because of my feelings of discontentment. My job was fine, my boss was wonderful, my coworkers became dear friends; but I was stuck in a job that didn't fit my passions and I was bored me to tears (some days literally). I was able to find other outlets for my gifts: writing during my breaks at work, leading a small group at the seminary; but I ached for more.

During that time of seeming inactivity, God was busy behind the scenes refining my strengths and preparing them. I yearned to write; He was growing me and stretching me so that I would later have something meaningful to write about. I longed to return to Asia to share His love; He was working in my personal life to give me skills I would need to survive there.

Are you a dreamer? Do you dream of quitting your job, jumping out of the boat and walking on water? Keep dreaming! When the time is right, and God opens your door, do not hesitate for a moment. Get out of that boat.

Our dreams are closely connected with our gifts and strengths and what God has wired us to achieve. As we grow in Christ our dreams reflect less and less any kind of false fulfillment (riches, fame, pleasure) and more and more the true fulfillment of knowing Him and using our talents in the way He has appointed to bring Him glory and to build His Kingdom.

If you are feeling discontent and unfulfilled in your work, start looking and praying right now for an outlet… somewhere on the side where you can use your gifts. Be 100% alert for what God might be teaching you that will enhance your gifts down the road. And dream. Dream big. Ask the Lord to make your dreams come true. He *will*. Finding your meaningful work is finding God's intended path for your life.

"Delight yourself also in the Lord, And He shall give you the desires of your heart." Psalm 37:4

If you are still discovering your gifts and strengths (and who isn't?) there are two books I cannot recommend highly enough. The first is *The Power of Uniqueness* by Arthur F. Miller Jr. and Howard D. Hendricks; the second is *StrengthsFinder 2.0* by Tom Rath (which comes with an access code for the Clifton StrengthsFinder test). Both of these books are priceless resources and will go a long way in helping you get to know the person you are meant to be.

Be forewarned that fear and shame are sure to be found hovering closely around our gifts and talents. If we ever struggle to believe our worthiness, the thought of actually doing what we love is daunting. *What if people don't understand? What if we're not good enough? What if we fail?* It feels safer to stick with the status quo and do things the way people expect them to be done.

Do not let fear or shame hold you back.

As Eric Liddell considered pursuing the Olympics, his sister urged him to keep on his path toward missionary work in China. Taking a wild side trip through long and rigorous physical training to the Olympic Games didn't match up at all with the expectations she held for her beloved brother. It didn't fit with what she thought the life of a committed Christian was supposed to look like.

Thankfully for the world, Liddell was able to quiet the well-meaning but misguided voices in his life and live out the unique life path God had in store for him. Eric Liddell ran in the Olympics for God's glory and the whole world watched in wonder. Liddell knew he was *worthy in Jesus.*

1. Based on what you have learned about yourself so far on your journey through life, what are those things which, when you do them, make you come alive? What types of things do you most love to do?

(To identify these things it may be helpful to think back through your life, including your childhood, and identify specific things you did that left you with a feeling of satisfaction and pride because you knew you did them well. Even the smallest event can speak volumes about your strengths.)

> "I believe God made me for a purpose, but He also made me fast! And when I run I feel His pleasure." —Eric Liddell (*Chariots of Fire*, 1981)
>
> "Every time people do something they experience as satisfying and as done well, they are in fact repeating part or all of a recurring pattern of specific competencies and motivations."— Arthur F. Miller, Jr. with Howard D. Hendricks, *The Power of Uniqueness*

2. When the author talks about "meaningful work" in this chapter, what does she mean?

3. How are you currently using your gifts, talents and strengths in your (official or unofficial) work?

4. Do you struggle inside because some of your gifts and talents are not being put to good use? Explain.

Identifying What's Stopping Us (pp. 113-114)

5. What aspects of the work you are doing now drain you most and perhaps do not use your strengths? What can you learn from this?

6. Is there work you feel you are "supposed to" be doing even though it is not in line with what you really want to do? Where do you think the "supposed to" message is coming from?

7. Read Psalm 139:13-18. Describe the intentionality and care God poured into designing you.

8. Read 1 Corinthians 12:4-31. Are there any ways you, perhaps a hand, might be trying to do the work of an eye or a foot?

9. God definitely calls us to work that is beyond us, work that stretches us and requires us to rely on Him. Does He ever call us to do something outside our natural gifting?

10. Are there any aspects of your current work (official or unofficial) where you may have confused compassion with calling and taken on something not actually intended for you?

Living the Dream (pp. 114-116)

11. What is your dream "slash career" description? (See page 114.) For example, King David's might have been Warrior/Shepherd/Poet/Musician/King. Your dream description may or may not include things you are doing now!

12. What is stopping you right now from pursuing the work that is most meaningful to you? What is one step you could take toward pursuing work that is more in line with your talents and strengths?

13. We Christians are just as prone as anyone else—if not more so—to put people in boxes labeled with our expectations and liberally tape them up with "supposed to's." Is there anyone in your life whom you need to release from your expectations and instead encourage to experiment with their strengths so they can bloom more fully into the special person God has created them to be?

GUIDEPOST #10
Questions for Reflection & Discussion

Laugh Till You Cry (pp. 117-118)

1. Describe the last time you laughed really, really hard. Who were you with? What were you laughing about? How did you feel afterward?

Live Your Soundtrack (pp. 118-119)

2. List several songs that have been especially meaningful to you at different points in your life. What was happening in your life when you loved these songs? What emotions does listening to these songs bring back?

3. What is a song that has meant a lot to you recently? How does it touch your heart? Bring a recording of it and play (or sing!) it for the group as time allows.

Dance With All Your Might (pp. 119-120)

4. How difficult is it for you to dance in front of other people? Looking back, can you put a finger on any factors/people/situations that played into how difficult or easy it is for you?

5. In what ways do you identify with the author's observation that many people struggle with the vulnerabilities of laughter, song and dance because of an inner struggle for worthiness and a subsequent need to be perceived as being "cool" and "in control"? (See pages 120-121.)

One of the most striking stories in the Bible is the story of King David, man after God's own heart, dancing nearly naked before the Lord with all his might, *in front of everyone.*

12 Now it was told King David, saying, "The Lord has blessed the house of Obed-Edom and all that belongs to him, because of the ark of God." So David went and brought up the ark of God from the house of Obed-Edom to the City of David with gladness. 13 And so it was, when those bearing the ark of the Lord had gone six paces, that he sacrificed oxen and fatted sheep. 14 Then David danced before the Lord with all his might; and David was wearing a linen ephod. 15 So David and all the house of Israel brought up the ark of the Lord with shouting and with the sound of the trumpet.

16 Now as the ark of the Lord came into the City of David, Michal, Saul's daughter, looked through a window and saw King David leaping and whirling before the Lord; and she despised him in her heart. 17 So they brought the ark of the Lord, and set it in its place in the midst of the tabernacle that David had erected for it. Then David offered burnt offerings and peace offerings before the Lord. 18 And when David had finished offering burnt offerings and peace offerings, he blessed the people in the name of the Lord of hosts. 19 Then he distributed among all the people, among the whole multitude of Israel, both the women and the men, to everyone a loaf of bread, a piece of meat, and a cake of raisins. So all the people departed, everyone to his house.

20 Then David returned to bless his household. And Michal the daughter of Saul came out to meet David,

and said, "How glorious was the king of Israel today, uncovering himself today in the eyes of the maids of his servants, as one of the base fellows shamelessly uncovers himself!"

21 So David said to Michal, "It was before the Lord, who chose me instead of your father and all his house, to appoint me ruler over the people of the Lord, over Israel. Therefore I will play music before the Lord. 22 And I will be even more undignified than this, and will be humble in my own sight. But as for the maidservants of whom you have spoken, by them I will be held in honor." 2 Samuel 6:12-22

Euphoric in the joy of God's blessing and consumed in worship of Him, David stripped off his clothes and whirled and jumped with all his might before the Lord. He danced with absolute abandon and utter disregard for anything or anyone except his God.

Back home in the palace, David's wife Queen Michal heard music and shouting as the people entered the city carrying the ark of the Lord. She moved to her window to observe the festivities and was appalled and disgusted at the sight which met her eyes. Verse 16 says when she saw her husband, the king, whirling and twirling in a linen ephod "she despised him in her heart."

As the festivities drew to an end, David returned to his family eager to share with them the joy of the day. Verse 20 says he desired "to bless his household." We can only imagine the spiritual high he was experiencing after such pure worship and after the triumphant events of the day.

However, he was in for a bitter surprise. What biting sarcasm waited for him as he walked through the door! "How glorious was the king of Israel today!" spits Michal in verse 20.

You should be ashamed of yourself. I am completely ashamed of you. Have you forgotten who you are? You are the king! When are you going to pull yourself together and act like one?

How often have we been brought crashing down to the dirt by someone's bitter words after we let loose and let ourselves go free?

More soberingly, how often have we spoken these cutting and judgmental words ourselves?

David's response is strong and sure and gives us a glimpse into the incredible secret to his ability to simply be himself and dance so freely and so hard before God in front of the people of his kingdom.

Look carefully at verse 20. He replies, "It was before the Lord, *who chose me.*"

It is because *He* chose me I play music and dance for Him. Because He *chose* me—watch out!—you will see me acting in even more undignified ways than this. Because He chose *me* I don't need to be proud and fake. I can be humble and be me.

Because *He chose me,* I am free. I don't have to try to impress anyone, I don't have to be "glorious." I am completely secure in who I am and the job God has given me to do.

Here we see a man who was absolutely 100% convinced of his worthiness. His sense of worthiness came not from his own efforts or performance or accomplishments but from the Lord God Himself *who chose him.*

David's belief in his unearned worthiness in Christ allowed him to let go. He discarded every pretense and every idea of what he was "supposed" to be or how he "should" act. He tossed aside every glimmer of a care about what anyone else might think about him and leaped and whirled himself before his God without holding back.

Who would you want to follow? A stuffy, stoic king stiffly waving to his subjects from afar to preserve his honor and so as not to dirty his robe? Or a king who threw it all off and danced his heart out before his God with all his people, inspiring everyone around him to live life to its absolute fullest?

Who would you rather *be*?

6. How does this story of David speak to your heart?

Letting Go to Be You (pp. 120-124)

7. Take some time to reflect about the different relationships in your life. In what ways have you hurt others, as Michal hurt David, by passing on a damaging message that others should be more "dignified," "cool" or "in control"? (See page 123.)

8. How can we help the kids in our life know that their worth isn't based on how "cool" and "in control" they are? How can we encourage them to keep singing and dancing freely all their days?

9. What are some specific steps (baby steps are ok!) you can take toward participating more fully in the joy and freedom of laughter, song and dance?

Closing Thoughts

10. Take some time to reflect on your journey through this book. What are you taking away with you as it draws to a close?

Works Cited

Brené Brown, The Gifts of Imperfection (Centre City: Hazelden, 2010).

Amy Carmichael, *If* (The Dohnavur Fellowship, 1938).

L.B. Cowman, *Streams in the Desert* (Grand Rapids: Zondervan, 1996).

Walter A Elwell, ed., *Evangelical Dictionary of Theology* (Grand Rapids: Baker Book House Company, 1984, 2001).

Matthew Henry, *Matthew Henry's Commentary on the Whole Bible.*

Lynn Hoffman, *Steps Into God's Grace* (2013).

Timothy Keller, *The Freedom of Self-Forgetfulness* (10Publishing, 2012).

C.S. Lewis, *Mere Christianity.*

Arthur F. Miller Jr. and William Hendricks, *The Power of Uniqueness* (Grand Rapids: Zondervan, 1999).

About the Author

 Leah Pritchard is a graduate of Moody Bible Institute with a degree in Communications. She and her husband Josh currently live and work in Asia with their two children Knox and Violet. A native of Vermont, Leah is always longing for mountains and loves being immersed in the beauty and stillness of nature. She finds her greatest joy deeply contemplating God's love and His Word, and cheering others on toward greater wonder and satisfaction in their relationships with Jesus Christ.

Made in the USA
Lexington, KY
22 September 2017